Net Numbers

A South Carolina Number Book

M is for Meg
R is for Riley
Count through South Carolina!
Carol Crane
2007

Written by Carol Crane and Illustrated by Gary Palmer

A special thank you to Catawba Cultural Preservation Project; and to Dock
and Amelia Skipper and Boykin Spaniel Rescue for photo references.

Sleeping Bear Press™

310 North Main Street, Suite 300
Chelsea, MI 48118
www.sleepingbearpress.com

© 2006 Thomson Gale, a part of the Thomson Corporation.

Thomson, Star Logo and Sleeping Bear Press are trademarks
and Gale is a registered trademark used herein under license.

Printed and bound in Canada.

10 9 8 7 6 5 4 3 2 1

Library of Congress Cataloging-in-Publication Data

Crane, Carol, 1933-
Net numbers : a South Carolina number book / written by Carol Crane;
illustrated by Gary Palmer.
p. cm.
Summary: "Using numbers, many of South Carolina's state symbols, historic
landmarks, and famous people are introduced. Topics include Boykin Spaniels,
Four Holes Swamp, and Carolina Mantids"—Provided by publisher.
ISBN 1-58536-202-6
1. Counting—Juvenile literature. 2. South Carolina—Juvenile literature. I.
Palmer, Gary, 1968- ill. II. Title.

F269.3.C72 2006
975.7—dc22   2005027797

For Pee Dee Reading Council, Catawba Indians at Rock Hill who graciously took time to help me with the history of their pottery, and the wonderful cooks at Beaufort who shared with me their frogmore stew recipes.

CAROL

❧

To my sons, Joel and Evan, my wife, Rebecca, and the people and places of South Carolina who made illustrating this book an adventure.

GARY

We hear the wagon coming,
coming 'round the bend,
bringing adventures to read,
stories we hope won't end.

South Carolina's books on wheels,
favorite tales and some brand new,
books about counting and history,
reading facts about our state, too.

In the early 1900s the first South Carolina bookmobile loaded books in wooden boxes and made monthly rounds of the county. The driver of the wagon would drop off one of the boxes of books for a family to read. The next month he would pick up the books and leave new titles. Most of the books were donated from libraries of doctors, judges, or a group of women who organized a library association for the purpose of establishing a public library. These women held bake sales and had other fund-raisers to buy books for the library.

South Carolinians were determined to have books for all people. Many of the first library buildings were small, abandoned buildings that the people repaired. Some libraries were upstairs in fire stations, police stations, or in the backs of stores. Today South Carolina has tax-supported libraries in all counties, and bookmobiles are modern vans equipped with many services and books for all ages.

one
1

1 mule-drawn wagon
carrying wooden boxes of books,
the first People's Free Library,
traveling to farms through fields and brooks.

Around 1905 a banker in Spartanburg, South Carolina, befriended a small dog that had followed him around town. He took the dog home and named him "Dumpy." He noticed that this little dog liked to retrieve balls or any other object that was thrown. The banker sent the dog to his longtime friend Whit Boykin. Mr. Boykin, when hunting, taught the dog to become a wonderful turkey- and waterfowl-retriever. "Dumpy" was the first Boykin Spaniel, which has been named the official dog of South Carolina.

The Boykin Spaniel has floppy ears, bright eyes, and a brown coat. He loves to hunt. He is small and has been known as "the dog that does not rock the boat." However, when not hunting, he becomes the family pet. Curling up in your favorite chair or on your lap, he will steal your heart.

two

2

2 Boykin Spaniels,
curled up in my favorite chair,
South Carolina's official dog,
our family's friendly pair.

The framework of our state
is a pattern of land, mountains, and sea.
Shaped like a triangle,
3 sides make our number **3**.

South Carolina is roughly 32,000 square miles in size. Land accounts for 30,000 square miles and another 1,900 square miles are covered by water. It is bordered by North Carolina to the north and Georgia on the south and west. The Atlantic Ocean is the eastern border. South Carolina is the fortieth state in size.

Another line runs across the state parallel with the Atlantic Ocean. It is in the middle of the state and is called the fall line. This line separates two distinct regions: the Upcountry (mountains) and the Low Country (beaches). There are sandy Midlands in between. Low Country is the home of plantations where rice and indigo were planted. Miles of white beaches, endless marshes, and nature tours bring tourists to relax and enjoy the resort islands. Upcountry has rolling hills, red clay earth, fast-moving streams, and lots of woods. The settlers that came to this area were farmers who found the right crops to grow. Looming beautifully beyond the Piedmont area are the Blue Ridge Mountains.

three
3

Four Holes Swamp is a swamp stream system in Calhoun County, South Carolina. It flows 62 miles through four counties before it joins the Edisto River and the Atlantic Ocean. Located in the swamp is the Francis Beidler Forest, a registered National Natural Landmark. This is the largest remaining virgin stand of bald cypress and tupelo gum trees in the world. Many of these giant trees rise out of black water streams and clear pools and have existed for over 1,000 years.

The National Audubon Society and the Nature Conservancy have raised enough money for this sanctuary to conduct educational sessions so that we may continue to learn from the area. While in the swamp you can see alligators, spotted salamanders (the state amphibian), snakes, owls, and if you stand very still, beautiful birds and butterflies. The early pioneers and the Yamasee Indians might have named the area Four Holes Swamp. The exact reason it is called Four Holes Swamp is not known.

four
4

4 spotted salamanders
resting on a log
in 4 Holes Swamp,
our state's famous bog.

A Catawba family of **5**—
  a father with children digging clay,
and a mother molding pottery,
    an ancient art still produced today.

The Catawba Native Americans settled on the banks of the Catawba River. They were called "People of the River." Living on a reservation in Rock Hill, South Carolina, these descendants are preserving their Catawba heritage. Catawba pottery is one of the oldest art forms still produced in South Carolina.

The men and children dig the clay from pits along the river. The women then clean the clay and grind it into a fine powder. They add just enough water so it is easy to knead. A piece of clay is flattened for the bottom. Then coils of clay are added, one on top of the other, to make the sides of the pot or vase. The coils on the inside and outside are smoothed with tools that have been handed down from generation to generation. The pot is left in the sun to dry, then put into an outdoor pit or open fireplace to make it watertight. The firing produces different colors.

five
5

Susie Simpson and her vice president of operations, Penny the dachshund, work making brooms in a 1740 slave quarters building in Boykin, South Carolina. School-children take field trips here to learn the art of broom making. Miss Simpson uses 100-year-old equipment from the Biltmore Mansion to hand make brooms. This antique wire holder holds the broom handle in place so wire can secure the corn straw. There were no instructions on how to use this antique machine, so she taught herself by taking apart old brooms to see how they were made. She boils the dye for colored brooms in a kettle behind the store. She hand carves some of the handles. Cutting the broom straw, soaking the straw, and then putting the handle in the machine is very time-consuming. It takes one and a half hours to make a broom. Her brooms have been shipped to 50 states and 24 countries.

six

6

6 straw brooms
of unique design,
a proud homemade heritage,
making floors in this country shine.

How Clemson Blue Cheese was made and cured in a mountain tunnel called Stumphouse is a time line of South Carolina's past that goes all the way back to a Native American legend. Stumphouse Mountain Tunnel in Walhalla was constructed to connect the port of Charleston to the Midwest. Its use was discontinued during the Civil War. Then a Clemson College professor discovered the possibilities of curing blue mold cheese in the tunnel. The tunnel is 25 feet high, 17 feet wide, and extends 1,600 feet through granite. An airshaft pulls warm air down the shaft, which combines with the cold air of the tunnel. From 1953 to 1956 this constant dampness in the tunnel was just right for curing blue cheese. Air-conditioning was installed at the college in 1958, and since then the cheese has been aged at the university. Today the cheese is aged for six months, processed, and wrapped by hand to be shipped all over the world.

seven
7

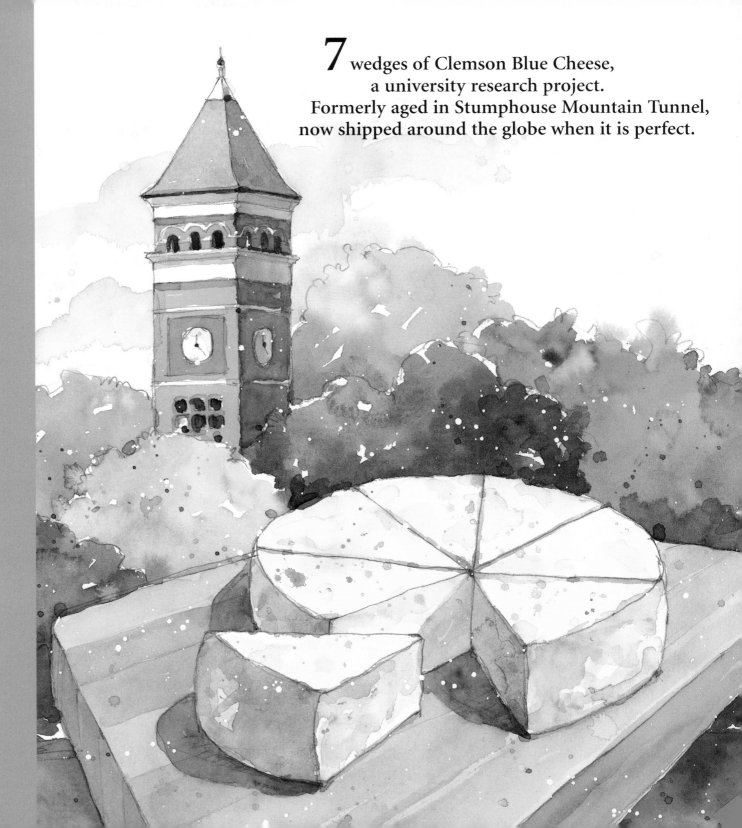

7 wedges of Clemson Blue Cheese,
a university research project.
Formerly aged in Stumphouse Mountain Tunnel,
now shipped around the globe when it is perfect.

The Carolina wolf spider was adopted as the state's official spider on July 21, 2000. It is the largest wolf spider in North America. Spiders are called arachnids. That means they have eight legs. Their legs are long and hairy. Their eyes shine green in the dark. They are night hunters and you can see them scurrying along in the dark. Some spiders spin webs and catch their prey in the silky, tangled, sticky mass. The Carolina wolf spider lives in a field or burrow. It listens for lunch to walk by its hole and then pounces. They eat large insects, even pinhead crickets. The female spider wraps 100 to 600 eggs in a silk sac. She carries the eggs around on her back until the spiderlings are old enough to escape from the sac. They climb onto their mother's back and hold onto special hairs for two months. The female spider lives about three years.

People who study insects and bugs are called entomologists. Would you like to study spiders?

eight

8

The Carolina wolf spider has **8** hairy legs and 8 shiny eyes. The largest wolf spider in the state, it horrifies and terrifies!

Philip Simmons was born in 1912 on Daniel Island, South Carolina. He moved to Charleston when he was eight years old. On his way to school he would walk by many blacksmith shops. He became interested in the work these men were doing. Blacksmiths are craftsmen who work on iron that is heated, hammered, and beaten into a desired shape. Have you seen pictures of blacksmiths shoeing horses? Philip Simmons became an apprentice (student) to learn blacksmithing. As years went by he opened his own blacksmith shop and started hammering out decorative wrought ironwork. He still works at his craft today.

When walking around Charleston you may see window grills, gates, stair rails, and ornamental fences. Many of these have been created by Philip Simmons. The ironwork looks black, but it is really green. This color, called Charleston green, is found throughout the city. The many designs he makes are of the natural world around him: the egret, palmetto tree, ocean waves, and magnolia leaves.

nine

9

9 iron window grills,
a Charleston art easy to identify.
Famed blacksmith Philip Simmons
shapes metal while sparks fly.

10 peach trees
planted in a row,
Upcountry peach blossoms
in a springtime glow.

The orchards of Upcountry produce peaches from June to September. Cherokee and Spartanburg Counties are famous for their mouthwatering peaches. In the spring the area is breathtakingly beautiful with peach blossoms. Roadside stands sell fresh peaches. Pie, cobbler, ice cream, butter, preserves, and pickles are ways to enjoy this fruit. Can you think of any peach desserts you love to eat?

Peaches are also found in the "Ridge" and the "Coastal Plain" areas. Peaches were discovered in South Carolina as early as the late 1600s, and by the 1860s the "tastier peach" was being shipped nationwide. South Carolina grows more peaches than their neighboring state of Georgia. Gaffney, South Carolina, has the Peachoid water tower. Families stop to have their photos taken below the huge tower that has been painted to look like the Palmetto peach.

ten
10

The Carolina Mantid is South Carolina's official state insect. This Tyrannosaurus rex of the insect world is native to North America. Two other mantids, the European and the Chinese, are thought to have been brought to North America around 1900 on a shipment of imported goods. Gardeners love to have mantids because they eat aphids, leafhoppers, and other unwanted garden pests.

The mantid's two front legs have sharp spines like a jack knife to attack its prey. The front legs, held upright, look like a human at prayer, giving it the name of praying mantis. It hides in twigs and leaves, camouflaging its body, and pounces on the unsuspecting insect from ambush. The female mantis lays up to 300 eggs and is one of the largest insects. Teachers bring praying mantises into their classrooms for observing. Have you ever had a mantis in your classroom?

eleven
11

11 Carolina Mantids,
insects with praying legs,
eat pests in gardens
and lay many new eggs.

12 Peanut Butter Benne Balls,
so easy to eat and fun to make,
a Bantu people's heritage—
    a delicious Lowcountry keepsake.

The Bantu people of West Africa call sesame seeds "benne." In the early 1600s the slaves brought with them benne, or sesame seeds, to South Carolina. The plant still grows in South Carolina today. The South loved these little nutty-flavored seeds that found their way into many cooking recipes. Traditionally, the sesame wafers are a Kwanzaa treat. Peanuts also came to South Carolina from Africa.

Maybe you would like to try this no-bake recipe:

- 2 cups peanut butter
- 2 ½ cups powdered sugar
- 2 ½ cups powdered milk
- 2 cups honey
- 2 cups sesame seeds

Mix the first 4 ingredients together in a bowl. Shape the dough into 1-inch balls. Spread the 2 cups of sesame seeds in a pie pan with some more powdered sugar. Roll each cookie around in the powdered sugar and seeds. Chill the cookies in the refrigerator and then enjoy.

twelve
12

The Park Seed catalog just arrived,
a favorite spring magazine.
Digging, mulching, and planting
packets of seeds are number **13**.

George W. Park was interested in gardening and flowers as a young boy. His mother helped him start a small garden of his own. Today the George W. Park Seed Company, Inc., located in Greenwood, South Carolina, is one of the largest horticultural seed companies in America. In 1871 he started a monthly magazine *The Floral Gazette* that offered advice on gardening. Readers were able to write in and exchange ideas and often traded plants, bulbs, and seeds through the magazine. By 1918 the circulation of the magazine was 800,000 customers.

In 1984 millions of Park's tomato seeds were part of a NASA space experiment. The seeds were in orbit for five years. Then in 1989 the seeds were distributed to more than three million students in the United States for science experiments. Students were to track the growth and keep the Park Seed Company informed of the results. In 1997 the Atlantis shuttle launch again used Park tomato seeds, exposing them to deep space conditions for 10-14 days.

thirteen
13

Shag dancing is a lot of fun for families. The music starts and everyone dances on the beach sand or on a wooden pavilion dance floor. It is so popular that the Shag Dance was made the official state dance in 1984. The Junior Shag Dance Association was established so the Shag Dance will always be a part of South Carolina History. All ages learn to dance the shag when the music plays. Shag dancing started on the beaches of South Carolina. The footwork has to be smooth and close to the ground so sand is not kicked into your partner's face. Some names of the steps are Belly Roll, Boogie Walk, or Sugarfoot. Kids as well as adults come to dance the shag in bathing suits or very casual dress. Let's dance!

fourteen
14

14 Shag Dancers,
 our state's official dance.
  Families dancing on the beach—
   kids, cousins, uncles, and aunts.

In the early twentieth century South Carolina was a major supplier of asparagus. It is a mystery how this crop grew here on thousands of acres.

The plant grows well along riverbanks, shores of lakes, and salty seacoasts. South Carolina has the right temperature for a long growing season. Asparagus is a member of the lily family. It is a perennial (yearly) plant that will produce up to 35 years. Williston, South Carolina, was called the asparagus capital. For many years during two months in the spring, Williston was a busy place with cutting, trimming, packing, and shipping asparagus to all parts of the United States. Aiken, Barnwell, and Bamberg Counties were the major asparagus production counties.

fifteen
15

15 spears of asparagus,
tied together and sold in a bunch,
a mystery crop of this state,
good for dinner and for lunch.

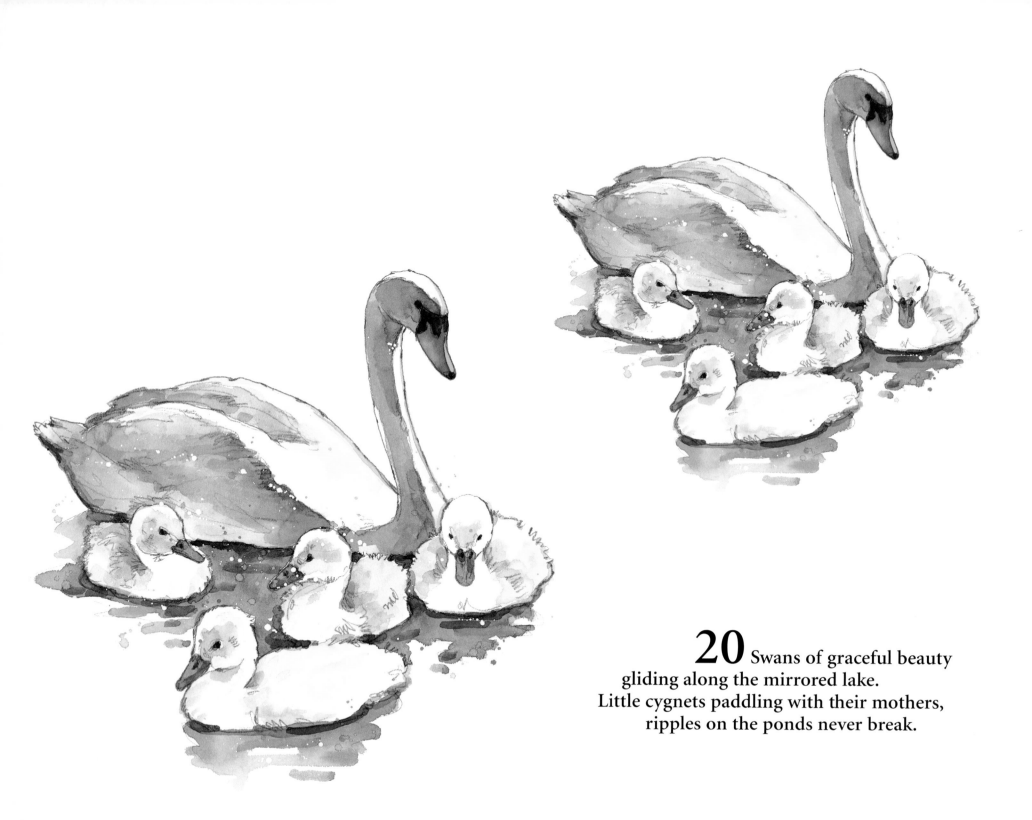

20 Swans of graceful beauty
gliding along the mirrored lake.
Little cygnets paddling with their mothers,
ripples on the ponds never break.

Swan Lake Iris Gardens in Sumter, South Carolina, has an international residence of swans in a beautiful botanical garden. In 1927 a local businessman was landscaping the grounds of his home with Japanese iris. They would not grow. He had his gardener dig up the bulbs and throw them into a nearby swamp. The following spring the iris bulbs burst into bloom. After years of land donations, a park was created and is operated by the city of Sumter. The black water of Swan Lake is dotted with islands and wildlife. This public park has eight different species of swans from around the world. A male swan is a cob, a female is a pen, and the young are called cygnets.

Swans like wetlands and land surrounded by water, where they build their nests on mounds. When the pen lays her eggs, she watches over them and will hiss and flap her wings if you try to get too close. Swan Lake is a perfect location for all these swans and their babies.

twenty
20

Any South Carolinian who thinks about a cookout immediately starts the fire and gets out the big stew pot. Friends and neighbors bring freshly caught seafood or anything else they may have on hand. The crabs and shrimp are taken out of their shells and put into boiling water with 2 dozen ears of corn and 10 pounds of sausage and potatoes. A large picnic table is covered with oilcloth and paper. When the stew has boiled, it is dumped out on the table and everyone digs in to the seafood and vegetables of this state dish.

Frogmore Stew's history dates back many years. State historians think it started with the slaves who brought their recipes from Africa. In later years, it is thought to have come from the shrimp boats that came in with a big catch. Wherever it came from, it is a wonderful part of the Low Country culture.

twenty-five

25

South Carolina's Frogmore Stew is number **25**.
Throw everything into the stewpot;
10 pounds of crabs plus 15 pounds of shrimp
and anything else that has just been caught.

From 1910 to 1996 the Laurens Glass Works of South Carolina provided beverage bottles for soft drink companies along the East coast and even as far away as Texas. Coca Cola, Dr. Pepper, and Pepsi bottling companies were important customers of the Laurens Glass Works. With the rapid growth of the company, many experienced glass blowers emigrated to South Carolina from other countries. Today glass bottles are made by machinery.

30 home-blown bottles
of various designs,
a taste of history in our state,
with the Laurens Glass Work's sign.

thirty
30

40 "Blue Row" Houses
built for families in Graniteville,
painted to match the stone
used for the South's first cotton mill.

In 1845 William Gregg founded the South's first cotton mill and started the textile industry in this state. The South was shipping raw cotton to the North. The state then bought textiles back from the North that could have been manufactured in South Carolina and other southern states. He built the mill of local blue granite and called it Graniteville Manufacturing. Today it operates as Avondale Mill. Mr. Gregg provided housing for his workers, a church, and a library. He built a school for children, and also provided teachers for the school. He fined parents five cents a day, which he withheld from their wages, if they did not send their children to school.

The mill village homes were painted blue and some of the "Blue Row" homes can still be found in the area today. He cared for his workers and they became responsible and proud of the village they lived in. William Gregg was inducted into the South Carolina Business Hall of Fame in 1985.

forty
40

50 Continental Soldiers plus hundreds more
with overmountain men and militia joining, too,
secured the "Battle of Cowpens" victory,
a Revolutionary War breakthrough.

The "Battle of Cowpens" (an Upcountry frontier pastureland) became the turning point of the Revolutionary War in the South. The American Patriots joined together with overmountain men to fight the British. These were soldiers from the mountains of Virginia, Tennessee, and North Carolina. They had fought at King's Mountain and came to help fight at Cowpens. General George Washington selected Nathanael Greene to command the southern patriot army. Nathanael Greene split his army and sent General Daniel Morgan to hamper and disrupt the British army. General Morgan played a cat and mouse game of battle with the British commander Lt. Colonel Banastre Tarleton. After one hour of battle the British army was defeated and the "Battle of Cowpens" became the turning point of the Revolutionary War for the American Patriots. The Cowpens National Battlefield is part of the National Park Service and is located north of Spartanburg, South Carolina.

fifty
50

In groups of 10 the children sit in a circle and read their favorite books. The next day the children pass the books to the right and receive books from the group on the left. Every summer libraries in this state have reading marathons (an event, session, or activity characterized by great length or effort). Children read for fun, knowledge, and speed to see how many new adventures they can read.

A very famous author, Peggy Parish, lived in Clarendon County, South Carolina. She wrote the Amelia Bedelia series of children's books. Have you ever read any of her books? Who is your favorite author?

100 Children in a reading marathon
in libraries, schools, bookstores, and homes,
discovering stories about science and art,
biographies, great adventures, and poems.

one
hundred
100

Carol Crane

Carol Crane is the author of 11 books with Sleeping Bear Press. In addition to *Net Numbers: A South Carolina Number Book*, she has also written *Wright Numbers: A North Carolina Number Book*; *Sunny Numbers: A Florida Counting Book*; and *Round Up: A Texas Number Book*; as well as alphabet books for Florida, Texas, Alaska, Georgia, South Carolina, North Carolina, Alabama, and Delaware. She is also the author of *P is for Pilgrim: A Thanksgiving Alphabet*.

Carol is a historian and has always been a journal writer. She loves to stop and read historical markers. Traveling around the country, she speaks at reading conventions and schools, networking with children and educators on the fabric that makes up the quilt of this great country. Using information in the state books, she transports kids around the states. Carol's greatest joy is to have a child say, "Wow! I didn't know that."

Gary Palmer

Gary Palmer, born in Alabama to a military family, was raised all across the United States and in Europe. He began showing an interest in drawing as early as five years of age. While residing in Key West with his family he began painting scenes on driftwood and selling them to the local tourist shops. From those meager beginnings Gary has pursued a successful career in illustration.

After attending Ringling School of Art in Sarasota, Florida, Gary moved to North Carolina with his wife, Rebecca. They have two sons, Joel and Evan. Traveling in and around the beautiful state of South Carolina from the Grand Strand to the foothills of the Blue Ridge led their two sons to attend Clemson University, one of the state's finest traditions! Gary's illustrations have appeared in national advertising campaigns, magazines, and corporate promotions. He has illustrated corporate art for South Carolina's Mead-Westvaco, murals for the North Carolina Museum of Natural Science, promotions for the North Carolina Zoo, and prints for the North Carolina Nature Conservancy. *Net Numbers: A South Carolina Number Book*, is Gary's third book with Sleeping Bear Press, and another opportunity to get out and explore the interesting people and places of South Carolina.